Introduction

D1756804

This guide covers the southern half of mainland Argyll, from the village of Inveraray in the north to the Mull of Kintyre in the south. It is a long, narrow stretch of land, with the long fjord of Loch Fyne and Kilbrannan Sound to the east, and the Sound of Jura – with the islands of Islay and Jura (see *Walks Islay, Jura & Colonsay* in this series) beyond – to the west. The peninsula of Knapdale and Kintyre is effectively a breakwater, protecting the waters of the Firth of Clyde from the storms of the Atlantic.

The land is mostly rough and hilly, though lacking the high hills found elsewhere in west and north Scotland. There are pockets of farmland (notably around Crinan and in the flat lands west of Campbeltown), but overwhelmingly this is a landscape of low, heathery hills, covered in places by extensive commercial conifer forests. There are some coastal cliffs around the southern tip of Kintyre (*Walk 28*), but the coast is generally low and gentle, with wide sand beaches at Machrihanish (*27*). To the west of Kintyre is the low, green island of Gigha (*22,23*).

i	Visitor Information Centre
– – –	Ferry Route
‥‥‥	The Kintyre Way

The nature of the walking in the area is as this description might suggest. There is a long distance path running the length of Kintyre (The Kintyre Way: a series of linking paths, tracks and roads running 100 miles/161km from Tarbert to Machrihanish), but most of the walks are relatively short: low hill climbs, forest walks and gentle coastal paths.

The population is small, and scattered through numerous settlements, mostly along the coast. The major centres are Lochgilphead and Campbeltown (*25*) (the latter is the largest, with a population of around 5,000). Other significant settlements include Ardrishaig (at the east end of the Crinan Canal) (*12*), the handsome old fishing port of Tarbert (*20,21*) and Inveraray (*1*). Transport links are simple: one main road runs up Kintyre and Knapdale, from Campbeltown to Lochgilphead. There it splits, with one road continuing up the coast to Oban and the other leading through Inveraray and on to Loch Lomond and Glasgow. There are also ferry links to Cowal and Arran, and to the islands of Gigha, Islay and Jura to the west.

The area is rich in history – and, indeed, in prehistory. The most dramatic example of this is Kilmartin Glen (*10*), which holds one of Scotland's most important collections of neolithic and Bronze Age remains. The area was clearly of great significance from earliest times, and the glen contains a mass of standing

Cup and ring marks, Ormaig (Walk 7)

stones, burial cairns, 'cup and ring' marked rocks and other evidence of early occupation. Information about this aspect of the area can be found at the museum in Kilmartin, while there is a splendid example of cup and ring marks at Ormaig (*7*).

The second great historical site is at Dunadd (*8,9*), where a low, craggy hill rises from the narrow waist of low land at the north end of Knapdale. The site must always have had obvious defensive virtues, but its particular claim to fame is as the principal seat of the kings of Dalriada – the chiefs of the Gaelic-speaking 'Scotti', who subsequently gave their name to Scotland. It was a centre of significance from the 6th to the 9th centuries and is best known now for the footprint incised on a rock near the top of the hill – believed to have been a part of the kings' coronation ritual.

When the area emerges from the largely hidden world of early history, it is as a part of the Highland clan system. Though there were a number of significant clans in the area – the MacDon-

Inveraray Castle
(Walk 1)

alds in Kintyre and the McNeills of Gigha and at Taynish (*16*) amongst them – the most important family by far were the Campbells. From their stronghold on Loch Awe, they moved south to Inveraray in the 15th century, and then gradually extended their grasp until they controlled most of the area covered by this book.

Inveraray is the quintessential Campbell town. The Earls (later Dukes) of Argyll lived at the castle (as they still do). The current building was built in the second half of the 18th century, when they were at the height of their wealth. Defence was no longer a consideration, and the building is essentially a house rather than a castle – though with added Gothic detailing as a nod to the family's long history. Inveraray itself is an architectural gem: a whitewashed planned village on the shore of Loch Fyne, built from new in the 18th century.

The most significant structure built in the modern era is the Crinan Canal (*9,11,12*): a 9-mile/14km link completed in 1801 to allow shipping to pass from the Clyde estuary to the west coast without having to pass around the perilous Mull of Kintyre. This picturesque canal is now almost exclusively used by yachts, passing through to the pretty village of Crinan (*11,12,13*), then on to the cruising grounds around Loch Linnhe, Mull and beyond.

Boats of a different kind were important to the 19th-century development of the area. The herring boom of that period brought great wealth to the coastal communities, when the fleets of skiffs based at Tarbert (*20,21*) and other villages provided cheap nourishment for the growing population of Glasgow.

This is a beautiful corner of the country, less well-known than most and therefore quieter for the visitor. This guide should help you to start your exploration. Happy walking!

Loch Fyne Skiff

1 Dun na Cuaiche

A straight climb, through mature woodland before reaching the open top, from the historic Inveraray Castle to the folly and viewpoint which overlook it. Length: **3-4 miles/5-6.5km** (there and back)*; Height Climbed:* **660ft/200m**.

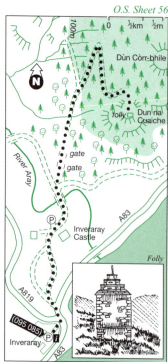

O.S. Sheet 56

This brisk climb can be started either from the whitewashed village of Inveraray or from Inveraray Castle itself. Either way there will be a charge for parking. The longer distance shown above assumes you are starting from the village.

From Inveraray, follow the A83 to the northern edge of the village then turn left up the driveway to the castle. After a short walk through parkland you arrive at the car park behind Inveraray Castle – the splendid 18th-century home of the Dukes of Argyll, which is well worth a visit on its own account.

Look away from the castle and you see a wooded hill with a tower at its summit. That is your objective. Walk out the back of the car park and head for the large stone bridge over the River Aray. On the far side, clear tracks go straight on and hard right. Ignore these and go half-right (an arrow marks the way), following a clear, rough path which climbs through fine mixed woodland.

You climb to a gate leading on to a narrow open area. Go straight across this to reach a gate leading back into the woodland. The track beyond climbs to a fork. Keep right (Dun na Cuaiche) and continue climbing.

The climb eases and the track reaches a hairpin bend. Double back to the right and follow the marked track/path up out of the trees and on to the splendid folly, built in 1748. The views south over Inveraray are stunning.

Return by the same route.

Two short waymarked walks through pleasant oakwoods on the side of Loch Awe. Can be combined to make one longer walk. Length: up to **3³/4 miles/6km**; *Height Climbed:* up to **330ft/100m**.

O.S. Sheet 55

To reach the start of these walks, drive north from Ford on the minor road up the west side of Loch Awe for a little over 8 miles to reach the village of Dalavich. The Forestry Commission's Barnaline Car Park is to the left of the road, shortly after leaving the village. A notice board in the car park shows the two routes.

The Red Route (Oakwood Trail) is a 2 mile/3.2km circuit which runs south from the car park through some fine ancient Atlantic oakwood. To follow it, look for the red marker post to the right of the notice board.

The route, on clear paths and forest tracks, takes you past a small pond and an old stable block before climbing to a bench with fine views over Loch Awe.

The Blue Route (Avich Falls Trail) is a 1¾ mile/2.8km circuit around the rapids of Avich Falls.

To follow it, walk out of the back of the car park, through a gate, and follow the forest track beyond. Just beyond a fenced enclosure a blue marker indicates the start of a path off to the right. Follow this, alongside the river and the series of long, low falls, to reach a footbridge. Cross this then climb to join a forest track.

Go right, then right again when you reach the public road to return to the car park.

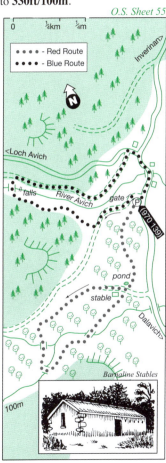

Barnaline Stables

3 Cruachan Tall Trees Trail _____ C

A waymarked forest walk passing a crannog site and some very tall conifers. Length: **2¼ miles/3.5km**; *Height Climbed:* **330ft/100m**.

This circuit starts at the Forestry Commission's Cruachan Car Park, 6 miles north of Ford on the minor road along the west side of Loch Awe. A map in the car park shows the route.

Follow the path (blue markers) out of the car park. Ignore a path coming in from the right and continue downhill to join a forest track. Go right, now parallel with the loch shore. Follow the track through mixed woodland. At a blue arrow just before a wooden bridge, go right (MacKenzie Grove) and follow a clear path through the tall trees to join a second forest road. Go right.

Just before a metal gate leading to the public road, go right again (blue) and follow a clear path to reach your outward route.

O.S. Sheet 55

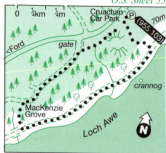

4 Moine Mhor _____ C

A tiny waymarked route, included because it leads, on duckboards, onto a remnant of the raised bog which once covered much of this area. Length: **⅓ mile/0.5km**; *Height Climbed:* **none**.

O.S. Sheet 55

'Moine Mhor' means 'great bog', and much of this area was once covered by raised peat bog: a dome-shaped layer of peat kept sodden by poor drainage. This environment is ecologically valuable, but only small pockets remain.

This very short walk leads through woodland and out on to the bog. To reach the walk, drive a mile south from Kilmartin on the A816 then turn right onto the B8025 road for Crinan. The car park is in the trees to the left of the road after a little over a mile. The route is self-explanatory.

5 Ardfern to Craobh Haven _____ B

A lineal route on metalled roads and good tracks, through farmland and woodland, crossing a wooded peninsula and linking two villages (and pubs). **Length: 6 miles/9.5km** _(there and back)_; **Height Climbed: 330ft/100m** _(both ways)._

O.S. Sheet 55

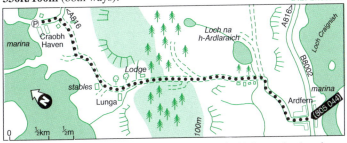

Ardfern is a small village on the north shore of Loch Craignish, most notable for its marina and boatyard. To reach it, drive 13 miles north from Lochgilphead on the A816, then turn west on the B8002 for a little over a mile.

Park near the marina and walk on along the road. Just beyond the primary school, turn right up the minor road signposted for Ardlarach. The road climbs through houses then swings to the right, climbing through farmland then descending towards a group of houses in a cluster of trees.

On the edge of the houses the metalled road ends, and tracks head to the right and straight on. Keep straight on, climbing past the houses towards a large conifer wood. As you approach the trees a track heads off ahead-right. Ignore this, and the track heading ahead-left just beyond.

The next ½ mile/0.8km is straight-forward: just follow the clear, straight track over its highest point then down the far slope. As you start the descent you pass an old ornamental lodge in the trees to your right. Immediately beyond this a track heads off to the right. Ignore this. Just beyond there is a further split. Keep right here, descending to cross a small burn then continuing down a glen of fine, mature woodland.

The track passes to the right of the imposing, castellated Lunga House (17th-century, in parts) and continues to a junction by riding stables. Go right here, following the metalled road across the slope, with fine views down over Craobh Haven to the islands beyond.

At a junction with the public road turn left, for a short distance, to reach the modern coastal village of Craobh Haven, with its marina and inn.

Having explored, return by the same route.

A short, lineal walk leading to a rocky headland. The paths are rough, wet or non-existent, but the views are terrific. Length: **2 miles/3.2km** (there and back)*; Height Climbed:* **230ft/70m.**

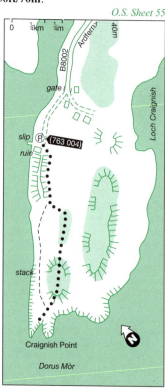

O.S. Sheet 55

To reach the start of this walk, drive 13 miles north from Lochgilphead on the A816, then turn west on the B8002. After a little over a mile you pass through the village of Ardfern, with the marina in Loch Craignish to your left. Continue along the winding, scenic road for a further 3 miles to reach a gate. Go through, close the gate behind you, and continue for a short distance to reach a small car park behind a slipway.

Continue walking beyond the car park. There is a rocky ridge running parallel to the shore. Walk along the left-hand side of this, keeping above a marshy area to your left for easiest walking. Step over a fence and continue until the bog to your left ends.

Looking across the low ground to your left you will see a path climbing up and across the slope. Aim for this and follow it onto a low ridge. Continue along the ridge. The walking is easy and the views – particularly west to the islands of Scarba and Jura, with the Gulf of Corryvreckan between them – are terrific.

The rough path descends from the end of the ridge and you continue out to a narrow, rocky bay and Craignish Point beyond. From here you look across the choppy waters of the Dorus Mòr to a group of rocky islands.

When returning, you can either retrace your steps or keep to the left and pick up a clear, rough path along a shelf above the shore. If you take this route you pass a fine rocky stack on the shore below.

A there-and-back walk, starting with a short climb to the terrific ruin of Carnasserie Castle, then continuing on paths and tracks, through forestry and open ground, to see some prehistoric rock art. Length: **6¹/₂ miles/10.5km**; *Height Climbed:* **750ft/230m**.

O.S. Sheet 55

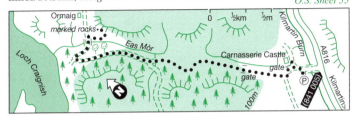

To reach the start of this walk, drive a mile north from Kilmartin on the A816 then turn left into the car park. A path from the back of the car park leads to a clear track, which winds uphill for a short distance to reach a signposted junction. You will go left here (Kilmartin) to reach Ormaig, but first go straight on for a short distance to reach the splendid ruin of Carnasserie Castle (late 16th century).

Retrace your steps to the junction and take the track for Kilmartin. You quickly reach a gate leading into a field. Go left for a short distance, then right, along the line of an old wall. At a gap in the wall turn left, through the gap, and follow the track across the slope for a few paces to reach a post. The main track goes ahead-left, down the slope. For this route, however, go right (there is a sign for Ormaig), up a grassy track. Climb to the top of the field, go through a gate then continue climbing, with a small burn to your right

and a wall beyond that.

The track goes through a low pass then winds down into the marshy glen beyond, eventually joining a large forestry track. Continue down this, with an increasingly deep, wooded den down to your right. If you look across the glen at this point you will see a path leading up to bare slabs of rock on a shoulder of the hill opposite – your destination.

The track reaches a junction at a hairpin bend. Double back to your right, down to a bridge over the burn. Immediately beyond the bridge there is an interpretative board to your right and the start of a path. This follows the burn for a short distance then climbs up to the bare slabs of rock.

The rocks are covered by a mass of early prehistoric carvings – mostly the so-called 'cup and ring marks'. No one knows their purpose, but similar designs can be found throughout Europe.

Return by the same route.

8) *A very short climb to one of Scotland's most historic sites: the remains of the fort which was once the capital of Dalriada. Length: ½* **mile/0.8km**; *Height Climbed:* **165ft/50m. 9)** *A complex circuit which may be walked in whole or in part, leading through woodland to the towpath of the Crinan Canal then back along quiet public roads plus a rough path by the River Add. Length: up to* **10 miles/16km**; *Height Climbed:* **165ft/50m.**

O.S. Sheet 55

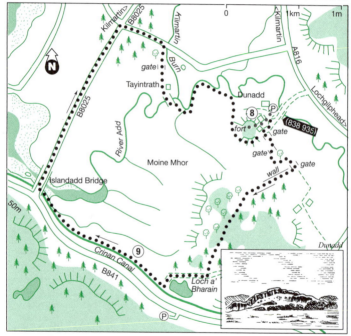

Dunadd is an imposing site: a rocky outcrop rising from the flat landscape of Moine Mhor ('the Great Moss' – now largely drained for farming) with the River Add meandering past.

When the moss was still undrained it would have added to the obvious defensive qualities of the site, which account for its historic importance. There was a fort on the site from

Iron Age times, but the particular significance of Dunadd is that it was the royal power centre for the kings of Dalriada – the land of the Scotti – from the 6th to 9th centuries.

To reach the car park for the hill, drive 4 miles north from Lochgilphead on the A816 and turn left at the sign.

Walk 8) The climb to the top of the hill is steep but very short. There are few signs of the structures which must once have stood there, but there is a stylised carving of a wild boar and an ancient Celtic inscription, plus – most famously of all – a carved footprint which may once have been part of the inauguration process for new kings. The views are excellent, too.

Walk 9) Walk back out of the car park and turn right (ie, away from the bridge) along a track. Ignore a track going right, up to a cottage, and keep straight on, passing through a gate. A few paces further on you reach a signpost, with a gate in the wall to your left. Go through the gate (the sign is for Cairnbaan) and follow the track beyond.

The track passes through a gate then climbs over a rocky outcrop. At the low point on the far side there is a gate with a signpost just beyond it. Go right here (Cairnbaan), off the track, crossing a large ditch then following a paved path with a reedy field beyond a wall to your right and trees to your left.

The wall eventually edges left, into what is now an oak wood, and the path follows it; climbing over a low ridge (the path can be wet at this point), then descending to join a forest track. Go right (Cairnbaan), down to and round the right-hand side of Loch a' Bharain (a reservoir providing water for the Crinan Canal) then climbing to join the towpath by the canal.

If you want to avoid road walking, retrace your steps from here. For a longer walk, head right and follow the towpath for 1½ miles/2.5km until the B8025 crosses the canal. At this point turn right, over Islandadd Bridge, and follow the straight road for 1½ miles/2.5km to reach a crossroads.

Go right here. After ½ mile/0.8km the road crosses the Kilmartin Burn. On the near side of the bridge, a sign points right for Dunadd. Walk down a rough track through mixed woodland; passing through a gate then exiting the trees onto reedy grassland. Looking ahead you should be able to see the small ruin of Tayintrath. Follow the clear path which passes to the right of the ruin then edge left, towards a bridge visible a short distance ahead.

Cross the bridge then go left, following the line of the River Add on a path through rough ground. The river meanders, and at one point the path leaves the bank to cut off a long bend. About a mile/1.6km from the bridge, as you approach Dunadd, the path leaves the river and passes through two fields to join a path around the south side of the hill of Dunadd. Follow this path back to the start.

Kilmartin Glen has the greatest density of ancient monuments in Scotland. This low-level walk, using paths, tracks and quiet public roads, visits a selection of the most impressive cairns and standing stones.
Length: **3½ miles/5km**_; Height Climbed:_ negligible.

The little village of Kilmartin is 7 miles north of Lochgilphead on the A816. It sits at the centre of a mass of prehistoric sites. For information on these, visit the splendid museum in the village.

Park in the car park beside the church and follow the pavement north along the main road for about 200m. Just before the garage, turn left through a kissing-gate signposted for Glebe Cairn. Cross the field to the cairn and information board, then continue across the field to reach a pedestrian gate. Go through this, edge right to cross a footbridge, then turn left along the path beyond.

After a few hundred metres take a path on your left to Nether Largie North Cairn (there is a hatch in a modern structure which allows you to enter the cairn), before returning to the main path and continuing to the next cairn. Beyond this the track leads down to Kilmartin Primary School, where it joins a quiet public road at a four-way junction.

Go ahead-right (Dunadd). After a short distance there is another cairn to your left. From this, follow a path signposted for Lady Glassary Wood across a field to reach a fine line of standing stones.

From the stones go right, back across the field towards the public road. When you reach the road, the

two stone circles of Temple Wood are visible just beyond. Turn right along the road and retrace your steps to the start of the walk.

O.S. Sheet 55

A terrific circuit, starting from Crinan Basin, running along the canal towpath, then climbing over a small hill covered with oak woodland (Woodland Trust). The views are excellent. Length: **2½ miles/4km**; Height Climbed: **260ft/80m.**

O.S. Sheet 55

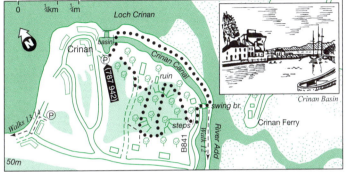

Crinan Basin

Start this walk from the pretty little village of Crinan, around the basin at the west end of the Crinan Canal. To reach it, drive 6 miles west from Lochgilphead on the A816/B841. Follow the road down to the end of the canal and park in the car park at the head of the basin.

Walk down the right-hand side of the basin, cross the canal at the lock gate and turn right along the towpath. This is a great place for looking at boats, but there is also a fine view across Loch Crinan to Duntrune Castle and the hills beyond.

After a little over ½ mile/0.8km you reach a swing bridge over the canal with a white cottage on the far side. Cross here and walk a short way along the road beyond, looking for a flight of stone steps leading up into

the trees to your right.

Follow the steep, rough path uphill through a fine wood of oak, rowan and hazel. The path passes a fine viewpoint then heads left and climbs to an even better viewpoint at the top of the hill. Continue along the path, which drops down the far side of the hill, then dog-legs right and continues to a four-way junction. Go right.

Walk down a shallow valley to reach another junction. A short diversion ahead leads to a terrace of ruined cottages, otherwise go left: climbing over a low ridge and descending to join a metalled road.

Turn right, towards a red-roofed cottage. Just before the cottage a sign points left, and a path leads over another small ridge then winds down through the trees to Crinan Basin.

*A splendid towpath walk providing pleasant, level walking. Few people will walk the whole length, but it can be joined at a number of places and gives fine views of the locks and the boats passing through. Length: up to **8¹/₂ miles/14km**; Height Climbed: negligible. Possible links with Walks 9 and 11.*

O.S. Sheet 55

Canal walks are a specialist interest. There are no climbs, and navigation could not be simpler, but if you enjoy watching boats they are a joy. The Crinan Canal has the additional attraction of passing through some truly beautiful scenery.

The canal was built to allow boats to pass from the Clyde to the west coast without having to make a detour around the exposed Mull of Kintyre. It was completed in 1801 and has 15 locks which lift boats 64ft/19.5m above sea level as they pass across the low ground between Ardrishaig and the picturesque little village of Crinan. It was originally built for fishing boats and puffers, but is now largely used by yachtsmen.

The towpath can be joined at a number of points (*see* map). If you wish to walk the whole length, there are bus links between the ends of the canal, though this will require a change at Lochgilphead. If you only want to walk a short section, the western end is the more scenic (*see* Walk 11), with wonderful views across Moine Mhor (*see* Walk 4) to Dunadd (*see* Walk 8); over the tidal mud and salt marsh around the head of Loch Crinan to Duntrune Castle and the hills around Kilmartin; and west to the islands.

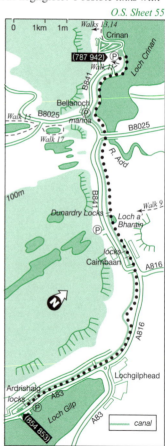

A modest climb, starting on rough paths behind the wooded shore, then climbing on forestry tracks to a fine viewpoint and the remains of a hill fort. Length: **4 miles/6.5km**; Height Climbed: **525ft/160m**.

O.S. Sheet 55

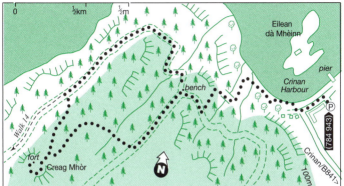

Turn off the A816 2 miles north of Lochgilphead and follow the signs for Crinan. As you approach the village, keep left on the road for Crinan Harbour. Drive down to the sea and turn right to reach the car park.

Walk back along the road to the bend where it joins the shore. A track goes straight on, into a house. Ignore this and head right, to walk along the head of the shore below the house. After a short distance the path edges into the woodland to your left and continues, eventually climbing away from the shore and up to a junction with a large forest road.

Turn right here and continue until you reach a clear junction, with a bench to your right. Pause to enjoy the terrific view then take the left-hand track (Forest Walk).

Follow the track through a shallow glen, climbing and then descending. Just after the road starts to descend, take a grassy path leading downhill on the right. This descends then climbs through a gap in a low ridge and heads left.

Follow this path to a clear junction. Your return route will be to the right, but first head left on a clear path to reach the ruins of an Iron Age fort at the peak of Creag Mhòr. The view from this point – including west to the north end of Jura – is superb.

Return to the junction and take the path indicated before. This descends through conifer woodland to rejoin the main forestry track. Turn right along this to return to the junction by the bench, then retrace your steps to the start.

Walks Inveraray & South Argyll

Grades

A
Full walking equipment –
including map and compass
– and previous hill walking
experience essential.

B
Strong walking footwear and
waterproof clothing required.

C
Comfortable walking footwear
recommended.

B/C, etc
Split grades refer to the fact
that the route described can be
walked either in its entirety or in
shorter sections.

NB: Assume each walk
increases at least one grade in
winter conditions.

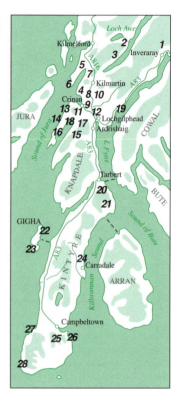

Published by: Hallewell Publications, Scotland
Printed by: J Thomson Printers, Glasgow

*While every care has been taken in the preparation of
this guide, the publishers cannot accept responsibility
for any loss, damage or injury resulting from its use.*

Walks Inveraray & South Argyll

A lineal route linking two coastal villages, mostly along clear tracks through conifer woodland but offering good views of the coastal scenery. Length: **7 miles/11km** *(one way); Total Height Climbed:* around **660ft/200m**, undulating throughout.

O.S. Sheet 55

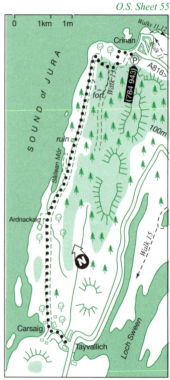

Turn off the A816 2 miles north of Lochgilphead and follow the signs for Crinan. As you approach the village, keep left on the road for Crinan Harbour. Drive down to the sea and turn right to reach the car park.

This route starts as Walk 13. Follow the instructions for that route as far as the junction with the bench. At this point, rather than going left keep straight on (Carsaig).

The track bends south to follow the coast. It passes a viewpoint with picnic tables before reaching a signposted junction. The path heading left (green-topped post) is part of Walk 13. For this route, keep straight on along the track.

After a further mile/1.6km, the track passes a small ruin then reaches a turning area. Beyond this the track becomes rougher and the woodland – until now predominantly of commercial conifers – more varied.

A short distance on a track heads off to the right. Ignore this and continue on the main track, which now drops to the shoreside at Sàilean Mór. The next 2 miles/3km are easily followed, as the track leaves the trees and continues across rough, open ground to reach the village of Carsaig.

Follow the road down through the houses to the little harbour. It is possible to return from here, but if you wish to visit the village

and beautiful natural harbour of Tayvallich, follow the public road half a mile/0.8km across the isthmus. At the village you will find a shop, a pub/restaurant and fine views across the moorings.

A waymarked circuit round a wooded inland loch where beavers may be spotted. Possible extension to the shore of Loch Sween. Length: **3 miles/4.8km** (for extension add **2 miles/3km**); *Height Climbed:* undulating.

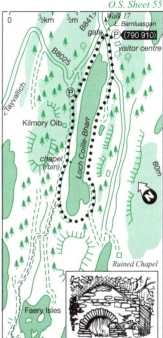

O.S. Sheet 55

To reach the start of this walk, drive 2 miles north from Lochgilphead on the A816 then turn left onto the B841. After three miles turn left onto the B8025 for Tayvallich. The car park is a mile along this road on the left.

A small visitor centre gives information on the project to reintroduce beavers to Scotland and you may be lucky enough to spot evidence of them on this walk.

Walk back out of the car park and turn right, down the public road. Almost immediately there is a gate on the far side of the road (red marker). Go through this and follow the clear path beyond, by the loch at first, then continuing through trees to reach a second car park.

Go left here on a forest track and follow it past a ruined township (Kilmory Oib) and a ruined chapel. Shortly beyond the chapel the track splits. Here you have a choice.

To reach the coast, go right (Faery Isles). A there-and-back diversion of 2 miles/3km leads down forest tracks to a magical spot at the head of Loch Sween. **NB**: this diversion is not waymarked and some map work may be needed.

To continue on the Loch Coille -Bharr Trail, keep straight on. At the foot of the loch the track gives way to a mix of rougher paths and tracks running back up the side of the loch. The route is well waymarked and never in doubt. Viewing platforms have been placed at intervals where evidence of beavers may be seen.

The path eventually joins a forest road then the public road. Turn left and follow the verge (being careful of traffic) back to the car park.

Ruined Chapel

A terrific sequence of rough paths and tracks leading through the oak-woods on a narrow peninsula. There are fine viewpoints from coastal sections, and from the bald peak of Barr Mòr (an optional extension).
Length: **6 miles/9.5km***; Height Climbed:* **330ft/100m** *(Barr Mòr). Leaflet available from car park.*

O.S. Sheet 55

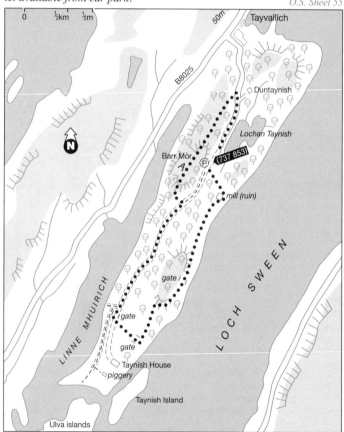

Taynish National Nature Reserve is an area of beautiful Atlantic oakwood on a narrow peninsula on the side of Loch Sween. There are colour-coded walks through the trees. This route is a combination of the various paths.

To reach the car park for this walk, drive 2 miles north from Lochgilphead on the A816 then turn left onto the B841. After three miles turn left onto the B8025 to Tayvallich. At the far end of the village, turn left onto a minor road (Nature Reserve). The car park is a mile along this narrow road and a rough track, just beyond the end of Lochan Taynish.

From the car park, look for the sign for Taynish Mill and follow a rough path down to the ruin of the old estate mill behind the shore. Having explored this, look for an arrow marking the start of the next stage of the walk.

An undulating path now runs down the peninsula through wonderful broadleaved woodland of oak, birch, hazel, etc. After about half a mile/0.8km the path reaches a gate in a stone wall. Go through this and continue, still in woodland, until a fence joins to your right, with a gate in it marked by a yellow arrow.

Go through this and walk across the field beyond, with the roofs of Taynish House (private) visible down

to your left. On the far side of the field you join the track leading in to the house. Turn right along this, passing through a gate and continuing.

Looking down to your left you will see another track converging from below. When the tracks join you have a choice. A diversion back-left at this point leads down to the shore at two points (*see* map) – the furthest south point giving a fine view of the tide race between the headland and Ulva Islands. In addition, a spur path leads to the ruin of a fine old piggery.

Having returned to the junction, continue back up the peninsula on the main track. After a mile/1.6km you will reach a junction, with a path heading off to the left marked by a red square. At this point, you have another choice. If you want the quickest return to the start, keep straight on. If you have any remaining energy, however, it is well worth going left. A clear, steep path climbs through oakwood before emerging onto the open crown of Barr Mòr. The views are tremendous: down Loch Sween and across to the hills of Islay and Jura.

The path continues beyond, descending to rejoin the public road/track. Turn right along this, passing Lochan Taynish and continuing back to the car park.

1 *Loch Sween* 2 *Island of Danna* 3 *Linne Mhuirich* 4 *Islay*

17 Loch Barnluasgan _____ C

A short waymarked trail around a quiet inland loch, with a possible extension through the surrounding oakwoods. Length: **1-2 miles/ 1.6-3km**_; Height Climbed:_ **165ft/50m** (on extension).

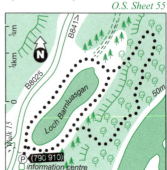

O.S. Sheet 55

To reach the car park for this walk, drive 2 miles north from Lochgilphead on the A816 then turn left onto the B841. After three miles turn left onto the B8025 for Tayvallich. The car park is a mile along here on the left.

There are two linked, waymarked walks (_see map_): a level circumnavigation of the little loch and a rougher, more undulating path through the beautiful Atlantic oakwood on the neighbouring ridge. Evidence of beavers may be seen on this walk.

18 Arichonan Township _____ C

A short there-and-back waymarked walk to a ruined township with fine views towards Loch Sween. Muddy in places. Length: **1¼ miles/2km**_; Height Climbed:_ **130ft/40m**.

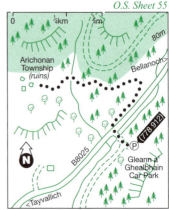

O.S. Sheet 55

This walk starts from the Forestry Commission's Gleann a' Ghealbhain car park. To reach it drive south from Bellanoch on the B8025. The car park is on the left after about 3 miles.

Walk back to the entrance to the car park and look for a yellow marker post at the start of a path on the far side of the road. Follow this clear path as it climbs, parallel to the road at first before swinging left.

The path goes through woodland at first before reaching the substantial ruins. An interpretative panel tells the history of the township.

Return by the same route.

*A waymarked forest walk through woods beside Loch Fyne. The paths are of varying quality, damp in places, but lead past some fine coastal viewpoints. Length: up to **5 miles/8km**; Height Climbed: undulating.*
The Forestry Commission leaflet to local walks is useful for this route, as there are a lot of paths in the wood and not many signs.

O.S. Sheet 55

To reach Ardcastle Wood, take the A83 Inveraray road from Lochgilphead. After 8 miles (shortly after passing through the village of Lochgair) there is a sign for the car park to the right of the road.

There are three waymarked walks through the wood (shown on the leaflet and on the information board in the car park). This route is the longest walk – the Ardcastle Point Trail, marked by yellow waymarks.

It is easy to get lost on the first stage. Follow the waymarked path out of the back of the car park and down to a junction. Turn right and follow the yellow markers. If in doubt at any junction, keep straight on to reach the shore of Loch Gair

then turn left. If everything has gone correctly, you should reach the ruin of little St Bride's Chapel and its surrounding cemetery.

From this point, the route becomes easier. At subsequent junctions, if in doubt simply follow the path nearest the shore. This will lead you past the fine viewpoint at Ardcastle Point then on up the shore of Loch Fyne through a range of different types of woodland.

1½ miles/2.5km beyond the point the path joins the route with blue waymarkers. ½ mile/0.8km further on the two routes bend away from the coast and make their way, through a number of junctions, back to the car park.

Two waymarked walks on the wooded slopes behind Tarbert. The walks follow good paths and pass a fine old ruined castle and several excellent viewpoints. Length: **1-3 miles/1.6-5km**_; Height Climbed:_ up to **590ft/180m**.

The handsome old fishing port of Tarbert sits at the head of little East Loch Tarbert, with the ruin of Tarbert Castle on the hill above. To reach the start of this walk, walk along the road on the south side of the harbour until you see a sign for Tarbert Castle to your right and a flight of steps.

Climb the steps to reach a metal kissing-gate. Go through this. To continue the walk you will be going straight on, to reach a second gate, but it is worth making a diversion to your left first to visit the castle: dating back to at least the 13th century, though the surviving tower walls date from the late 15th century.

Return to the path and go through the second gate, where there is a sign for Tarbert Forest. Follow the clear path beyond. After a short distance it splits. Keep left and continue until the next junction.

At this point you have a choice. **To complete the shorter walk**, go back-right and follow the path back to the first junction – though if you are planning to do this, it is worth heading left for a short distance to visit the splendid viewpoint overlooking the mouth of the loch.

To complete the longer walk, keep left at the junction. After a short distance there is a further split. A

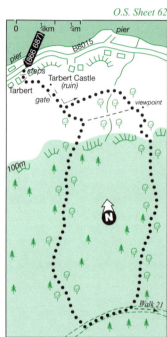

O.S. Sheet 62

short diversion to the left leads to the viewpoint, otherwise continue on the clear track through mixed woodland, climbing gently to reach a junction with a large track.

Go right here and continue until a clear path heads off to the right. Follow this back to the first junction.

*A lineal route on generally good paths, largely through conifer wood-
land but with sections over the open moor and through fine broad-leaved
woodland. The route ends are linked by a bus service, and Skipness
Castle is well worth a visit. Length:* **9 miles/14.5km** (one way)*; Height
Climbed:* **1200ft/350m.**

O.S. Sheet 62

The Kintyre Way zig-zags down the
peninsula, from Tarbert in the north to
Machrihanish in the south. This path
follows its most northerly section.

Start the route by following Walk
20 until, at the end of the penultimate
paragraph, you reach a junction with
a large track. Turn left here, along the
track. The junction is marked by a
signpost for the Kintyre Way.

For the next 3 miles/5km the route
is straightforward: climbing gently
along a clear track, initially with
views down to Loch Fyne, through
conifer woodland. Eventually the
track emerges onto heather moorland.

The track climbs further, with a
burn down to your left, then begins
to descend. Watch for a signposted
junction with a rough, grassy track to
your left. Turn on to this and follow
it across the moor to the edge of a
conifer plantation. Once amongst the
trees, the track weaves to the left then
begins to descend by a small burn.

At a junction with a large track,
go straight across and continue, with
views of Arran beginning to open up
ahead. Just beyond a picnic site
you go through a gate and continue,
now on a clearer track. Keep left
at a clear junction and continue for
2 miles/3km, through the pleasant
woodland by the Skipness River,
down to the public road in the little
village of Skipness.

The bus stop is directly opposite. A 1 mile/1.6km walk to your
left leads to Skipness Castle; a 2
mile/3km walk to your right, along
the B8001, will lead to the Arran ferry
terminus at Claonaig.

Gigha is a small island off the west coast of Kintyre. It is linked to the mainland by a vehicle ferry (though you scarcely need a car), and has a shop and a hotel/bar. There is plenty to explore, but these two walks should get you started. **22)** *A lineal walk along the quiet public road to the north end of the island, where there is a fine viewpoint and a sandy beach. Length:* **9 miles/14.5km** *(there and back); Height Climbed: negligible.* **23)** *A lineal walk, starting on the public road then continuing through woodland and farmland to reach a rocky bay. Length:* **5 miles/8km** *(there and back); Height Climbed: negligible.*

O.S. Sheet 62

Gigha Ferry

To reach the Gigha ferry, drive 19 miles south from Tarbert on the A83 and turn right at the sign for Tay-inloan. The short minor road leads straight to the car park and the ferry.

The ferry trip takes 20 minutes and ferries leave approximately every hour. Times can be checked at **www.calmac.co.uk**. Make sure to leave enough time to complete your walks and get back for the last ferry.

The island is small – 5 miles in length and about a mile across at its widest – but it has a long history. It has been inhabited since prehistoric times, and on your walks you will come across cairns, standing stones and the ruin of 13th-century Kilchattan Church. The island is associated with the Vikings (the name is assumed to be Norse, though its meaning is uncertain) and with Clan MacNeill.

Once off the ferry, walk up the public road. You pass the entrance to the Boathouse restaurant and continue up to the junction with the Gigha's 'main road' – the single road which runs down the length of the island.

Walk 22) To reach the north end of the island, turn right, past the shop, and simply follow the road. It is a 3 mile/5km walk along the quiet road, through fields and rough grazing land. Beyond Tarbert farm the coastal views begin to open out to either side.

Continue to a small, rough parking area marked by a sign for Eilean Garbh Twin Beaches. There are three short extensions from this point:

To reach the north end of the island, keep on along the road for a short distance. It turns right then left, passing a small ruin to your right. Immediately beyond this a rough path heads off to the left. Follow this uphill, through bracken, to reach an ancient cairn on a low hilltop. The views are terrific: west to Jura and Islay and north up the coast of Kintyre and Knapdale. Return to the parking area.

To reach the twin beaches, follow the direction indicated by the sign. A grassy path crosses a grazing area then loses itself in a thicket of scrub. Persevere and you will reach a low isthmus leading out to a rocky hill, with beaches on either side. The north beach is of fine sand, and this is an excellent place for a picnic.

To climb Cnoc nan Gobhar (the rocky hill immediately behind the parking area), just start climbing with the wall to your right, then turn left along the ridge.

Return along the public road.

Walk 23) For the south walk, turn left at the junction by the shop. You quickly pass the hotel and the start of a signposted path to your left (Rudh'a' ChinnMhoir) which leads down to a sand beach. Continue past houses and into the woods around Achamore House.

A sign points right for Achamore Gardens. Walk up this metalled driveway, passing the entrance to the gardens (open to the public, and with a fine array of rhododendrons) and the Village Hall, then continuing to the ruined Kilchattan Church and its surrounding graveyard.

Just beyond this the track forks. Keep left. After ½ mile/0.8km, as the main track heads right to the buildings at Ardlamey, a signposted track heads off to the left. Follow this grassy track across fields to an isolated cottage. Turn left on the near side of the cottage and follow a rough path down to a bay of sand, rocks and little islands.

Return by the same route.

A waymarked forest walk (including a section of the Kintyre Way), starting through trees before climbing onto the open hilltop and providing terrific views of east Kintyre and the Isle of Arran. Length: **3¹/₂ miles/5.5km**; *Height Climbed:* **660ft/200m.**

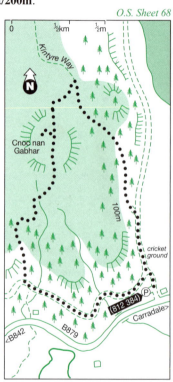

O.S. Sheet 68

Carradale is a little village clustered round a harbour on the east side of Kintyre, looking across to the Isle of Arran. To reach it, drive 14 miles north from Campbeltown on the B842 then turn right on the B879.

Just before the first house on the left there is an entrance to the left and a sign for the Carradale Cricket Club. Turn in here and you quickly reach a car park.

Walk on along the track beyond the car park. Follow the track up to a junction with another track, by the cricket ground. Go right, up the left-hand side of the cricket ground. Shortly beyond this the track forks. Keep left here. In a short distance the track becomes a footpath and begins to climb the slope.

After a little over half a mile/ 0.8km there is a signposted junction, with the Kintyre Way going straight on and Deer Hill Walk heading left. Go left and climb for a short distance, before the path turns left and runs level across the slope. Watch carefully for a spur path heading back-right. Make a diversion up this to reach the top of Cnoc nan Gabhar, from where there are wonderful views: across to Goatfell and the other peaks on Arran, and down Kilbrannan Sound to the granite plug of Ailsa Craig.

Return to the main path and continue. The path descends to join a clear forest track. Turn left along this to return to the junction by the cricket ground.

A waymarked forest walk, starting through fields then climbing, through mixed woodland, to a fine viewpoint overlooking Campbeltown. Length: **3 miles/5km**; *Height Climbed:* **330ft/100m**.

O.S. Sheet 68

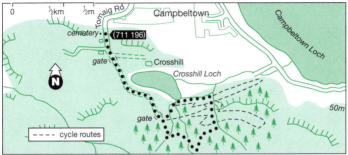

Beinn Ghuilean is a hill (1,161ft/ 351m) overlooking Campbeltown from the south, with a clear peak but flanks covered by conifer woodland. This walk does not climb to the top of the hill, but follows waymarked paths through the trees.

To reach the start of this walk, drive west from the centre of Campbeltown on the B842 (the Southend road). Near the end of the buildings Tomaig Road heads off to the left. Turn on to this and follow it for ½ mile until, just beyond the cemetery, there is a small parking area to the left of the road (please note, there is no other parking space here; if it is full, please park back in Campbeltown).

Walk on up the road to reach a right-angled bend. Keep straight on here, on a track. When the track heads left, almost immediately, to reach a farm, go through a pedestrian gate and continue along a rough track up the right-hand edge of a field.

Follow the track down towards the end of Crosshill Loch then back up towards the trees, passing through a further three gates on the way. After the last gate, just before entering the trees, there are information boards showing the path (and cycle routes) through the wood.

The route is difficult to describe but easy enough to follow (it is marked by blue circles): up the slope, through mixed woodland, to reach an elevated point with fine views of Campbeltown, Arran, Machrihanish, Islay and Jura, then back down again. There are junctions with the cycle routes, but keep following the signs and it is clear enough.

Once back down to the gate at the edge of the trees, retrace your steps to the start of the walk.

A rough walk across a tidal isthmus to a small, steep-sided island. The length includes a shore walk to a cave containing a religious painting, and a climb to the top of the island. Length: up to **5¹/₂ miles/9km** (there and back)*; Height Climbed:* up to **360ft/110m** (if climbing the hill).

O.S. Sheet 68

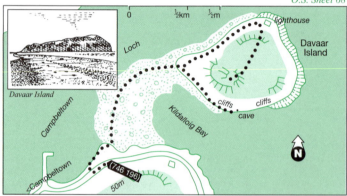

Davaar is the prominent island in the entrance to Campbeltown Loch – the enclosed bay with Campbeltown at its head. From the centre of the town, follow the minor road around the south side of the loch for just over 2 miles. Park in a layby on the left, a short way beyond the long pier.

The shingle spit out to the island starts to dry out about two hours before low tide. Check times online (**www.ukho.gov.uk/easytide**) or at the Campbeltown visitor information centre.

From the near end of the layby a path leads along the beach and out across the curved spit to the island. On the island, a vehicle track leads round to the lighthouse and there is an obvious path up to the summit of the hill. On your way to the top keep well clear of the cliffs on the south side of the island and watch out for the small herd of wild goats.

Return to the point where you reached the island and walk round the shore the other way – on grass at first and then there along the rocky foreshore. There are a number of caves in the high cliffs. The one you are looking for has a small sign by the entrance. Inside you will find a painting of the crucifixion: the work of a local artist, Archibald MacKinnon, in 1887.

Return by the same route, making sure you have left plenty of time.

A short, lineal, coastal walk from a small village. Starts by the public road, passes a bird observatory, then continues across grassland to a fine cliff-backed bay. Length: **2 miles/3km** (there and back)*; Height Climbed:* negligible.

O.S. Sheet 68

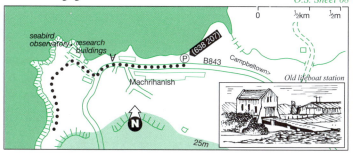

Machrihanish is a tiny resort village, due west from Campbeltown on the Atlantic coast of Kintyre. To the north of the village there is a long sand beach – 3 miles/5km – backed by dunes, famous golf courses and Campbeltown Airport.

To reach the village, drive 4 miles west from Campbeltown on the B842/B843. Park in the car park behind the shore, just beyond the club house for the Machrihanish Golf Club, then walk on along the road.

The start of the walk is through the village, with a string of villas to your left. Once the road leaves the village there is no pavement, but the road is quiet and there is a wide grass verge.

Looking west you should be able to see the islands of Islay and Jura, with Gigha to the north.

When the road leaves the shore, turn right at a junction signposted for the Seabird Observatory. Follow the track past the old lifeboat building and on until you are level with the Marine Research buildings. If you keep straight on at this point you will reach the Seabird Observatory (open to visitors). To continue with the walk, go left at a junction and follow an increasingly grassy path behind the shore to reach a beautiful bay with a shore of sand and rock backed by grassy slopes and low crags.

Return by the same route.

1 *McArthur's Head* **2** *Sgarbh Breac (364m)* **3** *Sound of Islay* **4** *Paps of Jura*

*A very short, very steep descent to a lighthouse on a metalled road –
followed by a steep return climb! The long drive in is part of the charm;
the views across to Ireland are terrific – make sure you pick a clear day
for the trip. Length:* **2 miles/3km***; Height Climbed:* **980ft/300m**.

O.S. Sheet 68

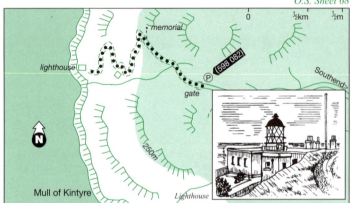

Lighthouse

To reach the Mull of Kintyre – the
south-west corner of the distinctive
Kintyre peninsula – drive 7 miles
south from Campbeltown on the
B842 road for Southend. A mile
short of Southend turn on to a narrow
single-track road. After a further 1½
miles turn right at a junction (signposted for the lighthouse) and follow
an undulating, winding road 7 miles
to the car park at its conclusion.

The route couldn't be simpler: just
go through the gate at the end of the
car park and follow the tarmac road
as it winds down to the lighthouse.
The views are terrific. It is only 12
miles across the North Channel to
Antrim in Northern Ireland. You can
also see Rathlin Island, where Robert
the Bruce allegedly had his famous
meeting with a spider. To the north,
you can see Islay and Jura.

On the way down, watch out for
a cairn – about 100m off the road, up
to your right. This is the memorial
to the men who died in the Chinook
helicopter crash in 1994.

The lighthouse itself is dramati-
cally positioned, though it has no tall
tower (its raised position – on top of
300ft/100m cliffs makes this unneces-
sary). The structure was built in 1788
and was manned until 1996.

When you get to the lighthouse,
take a rest. It is a steep climb back to
the car!